D1649460

Nightmare:
Two Ghostly Tales

Contents

Written by Berlie Doherty

Illustrated by Martin Ursell and Paul McCaffrey

Nightmare

1 "Stay with me!"

Rab isn't a house person. He lives with his grandad in a hut near the railway lines. He doesn't always live there; sometimes I don't see him for weeks or even months, and then he just turns up as if he's never been away. He isn't much older than me, but he knows everything. I'm sure that's because he isn't a house person.

His grandad's a grimy-looking, cold and sour fellow; he never speaks to me. I'm not sure I like him at all.

And when they feel like going, they just go. I hate it.
I never know they've gone. I go down to their hut and try
to peer in through the one high window, but they have
stringy curtains draped across. People have tried to get
that hut knocked down while they're away, but they can't.

It belongs to Rab and his grandad. It's their home.

"I wish you wouldn't go without telling me," I say sometimes. "I hate that, not saying goodbye and that."

It always makes him laugh. "What's the point of saying goodbye?" he says. "I know I'll be coming back."

And he always does. I see him leaning against the chestnut tree or sitting astride the wall near our house and I think, "Great! Rab's back!"

"Coming on moors?" he asks me as if I only saw him yesterday. "Coming up to Downpour?"

And before I know it, I'm racing over the moors with him, scrambling over those massive boulders that he says are fossilised dinosaur droppings, and slithering behind the waterfall to the dark cave that we call the Downpour Den.

"Cavemen lived here," he tells me. His voice bounces round the dripping hollows. "You're standing on the dust of their bones."

Last time Rab turned up was in the dead of last winter. I wish I hadn't seen him.

5

I was just going up our road and there he was, hunched up against the cold. The snow had come a few days before and now it was packed ice. It was an effort to walk upright.

"All right, Rab?" I shouted, pleased to see him but not showing it.

"Coming up to Downpour?" he asked.

"Eh, it's freezing!" I said. "We'll never get over moors in this lot."

"Get your boots on." He held his hands up to his mouth as though he was trying to melt his fingers with his breath. "See you at the stile. There's something I want to tell you."

I always do what Rab says. I can't help it. Half an hour later, I'd got my thickest clothes and my boots on, and I was standing by the stile that leads off up to open moorland, stamping on a patch of ice that was iron-hard. Nothing moved. The sun was lemon-yellow, but there was no heat from it at all, and the blades of grass and bells of dead heather were clamped in their own ice-shells.

I heard Rab whistle and saw him on the footpath. I waved and swung myself over the stile, lost my footing on the last slippery step and sprawled headfirst into the ice blades. I slithered after Rab, my heart jerking every time I lost my footing, and caught up with him at The Edge. He was sitting with his legs dangling over a drop of nearly 30 metres, looking out across the deep, white floor of the valley.

I eased myself on to the slab next to him. In summer you can hear the curlews up here, and the cackling of the grouse on the moors, and the sheep yelling to each other across the slopes, but today, there was nothing. Not a sound.

"Everything's died," I said.

He answered, not looking at me, "It's the shortest day of the year. Everything's standing still. The sun, and the grass, and the streams, and the birds. Nothing's moving."

"You'd think it was waiting for something."

"There's nothing to wait for now. It's too late."

You don't expect Rab to sound sad like that.

8

He spat over The Edge. We listened out for the tiny splat as it struck rock, and laughed. That was more like it.

"It's good for you," he told me. "Clears your passages. If you swallow your goz, it clogs up all your works."

He climbed over a boulder that was completely cased in ice, and then started running, his boots striking the iron of the ground like flints. We skidded down the slope to Toad Rock. From here the narrow track twists round below the waterfall. Usually you're deafened by the clamour; it drowns out everything, and the spray showers over you — no escaping till you ease yourself behind it into Downpour Den.

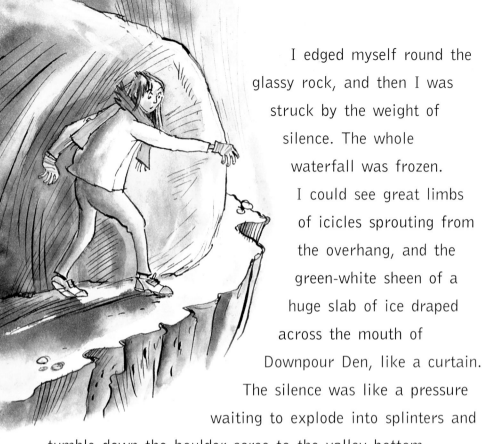

I edged myself round the glassy rock, and then I was struck by the weight of silence. The whole waterfall was frozen. I could see great limbs of icicles sprouting from the overhang, and the green-white sheen of a huge slab of ice draped across the mouth of Downpour Den, like a curtain. The silence was like a pressure waiting to explode into splinters and tumble down the boulder scree to the valley bottom.

Rab was clinging on to a rock near the overhang. When I reached him and looked up at the frozen curtain that hung over the Den, I saw something that was so terrifying that I'll never get it out of my mind, that I think of every day, as if it's part of me now. It was this: a horse, trapped in the ice. A great black horse, its legs straddled and its hooves frozen to the rock, its head lifted, teeth bared in fright, its eyes staring; locked in death.

10

11

I think I crawled back up on my hands and knees until I felt safe enough to stand, and then I started running, feet splaying out each side of me. I turned round but Rab was nowhere in sight. I waited a bit, but the cold began to seep into me. Rab knew many routes over the moors – he could be anywhere.

I jogged back home, glad of the comforting warmth of our house, and of the quiet, normal talking of my mum and dad in the kitchen.

I couldn't sleep that night. I went downstairs and
wandered into the back room. I thought I'd like to look at
the moors in the moonlight, the blue-white gleam of the
snow. Just before I reached the window I heard Rab's
voice, calling me softly from outside. It was almost as if
I'd known he'd be there. I tugged at the curtain.

There, instead of the window, was a huge slab of ice, and frozen into it, the black horse.

Its eyes were wide open and its ears pressed back, and its yellow teeth were bared in fright. As I watched in the same lock of fear, it reared back its head. In slow motion its front legs carved an upwards arc and flung black hooves to pound against the ice. I could hear it tearing in front of me, above and around me, splintering and crinkling as a thousand tiny shards showered over me, sharp as glass, bright as water.

Hooves flailed as the black horse reared again, hot life snorting from its nostrils. And clinging on to his back, laughing down at me, was Rab.

"Come on!" he shouted. "Up on moors." He leant down and heaved me up.

I can feel the way my legs ached as they stretched across the black sinewy back, and the lurching sensation beneath me as we galloped over the moors. I dug my fingers into Rab's coat, and clung on. The air on my cheeks was raw. We plunged on into the black bitter night, away from the houses, away from the lights.

I felt as if all my known world was slipping away from me, and that this was where I'd rather be; riding forever in cold air. We soared over the white stile at Moorgates and thundered up the tracks, with the stars hanging and turning like icicles. Gleaming boulders loomed up and away. We were streaming fast, floating; we were in a different element, like water.

I recognised the squat bulk of Toad Rock. I recognised
the splintered ice-curtain of the Downpour, and as the
horse leapt towards the black cavern behind, I tried to
slide off his back.

"No!" I screamed. "Not there!"

Rab's laugh echoed and bounced in the hollows of the
cave. "Stay with me," he urged. "Don't leave me."

I heard a creaking above my head; the slow languorous
curtain of ice sliding down to envelop the cave. I felt the
intense chill as it scraped across my skin, trapping me.

2 "It's too late!"

My dad found me standing shivering in the dark of the back room.

"You've had a nightmare," he said. "You're all right."

I jerked back the curtain, expecting to find the window shattered and the snow on the lawn outside swirled round with the kicking of hooves, but there was nothing to see, only the moors quiet and cold in the moonlight, and the stars like twisting icicles.

"There was a horse," I told Dad. "It carried me off to the Downpour ..."

He led me back upstairs to my room. "People used to think", he told me, "that wild horses came in the night and carried them off to terrifying places. That's why it's called a nightmare. Go to sleep now. You'll be all right."

But I had no intention of sleeping ever again. I sat bolt upright in my bed with the light on, listening out for the stamp of hooves on the iron earth, and for Rab.

It stayed just below freezing all next day, but the sun was bright and the sky was a fierce blue. I couldn't get Rab out of my mind. I wanted to tell him about my dream. Why had he laughed? Why had he wanted to be trapped in the ice cave, when I'd been so frightened?

And even as I thought of all the things I wanted to ask him about, the feeling came to me just as powerfully as it had done last night, that it hadn't been a dream at all, but that it had really happened.

And there was another thing that bothered me. When we'd gone up to the Downpour yesterday, he'd said there was something he wanted to tell me. He'd taken me to see the horse, but he hadn't told me anything, except that it was the shortest day of the year. "*It's too late.*" That was what he'd said.

By the time I left school, it was nearly dark. I turned down towards the railway track. It was bitterly cold down there, with the icy wind coming straight off the moors. I picked my way along the path. A stray cat yowled at me from its ratting place near a heap of rotted compost. I found my way to the high bulk of Rab's hut. It was all in darkness.

I went up to it all the same, and tried to peer in through that high, curtained window. Surely they hadn't gone again so soon?

I was just about to walk away when I heard a movement inside; a kind of hollow knocking.

"Rab?" I shouted. "You in there?"

There was silence, but then the knocking came again; but it wasn't knocking at all, it was the stamping of hooves.

I backed away, and the stamping began again, more urgent this time. The high wooden door of the hut shook, and I knew that the horse inside was rearing up against it, beating its hooves, trying to tear it down.

"Stop it!" I shouted. "I know what you are. You're not a real horse at all. You're only a nightmare."

I started to run, skidding down the slippery path. But how could it be a nightmare, when the lights of my town were blinking like yellow stars in front of me and I could hear the drone of cars? Behind me I heard the thundering of hooves on wood, and a terrible splintering as the door began to give way.

I ran wildly, slipped on the ice and fell headlong.

"You all right? Come on, now, up you get. No bones broken." Davey Brown, an old friend of my dad's, hauled me on to my feet. "You're shaking like a plate of jelly. Shouldn't run on ice, you know."

"I saw a horse," I said. "It scared me."

"A horse?"

"I didn't exactly see it. I heard it, down by the railway lines."

He shook his head. "I doubt it. Whereabouts was it?"

"I thought I heard it," I said, "in the hut."

"But there isn't a hut," Davey said, "not any more."

Not any more.

I began to shiver violently again.

"They pulled it down over the weekend," Davey went on. "Real eyesore, that thing was."

"But it's their home! They live there."

"Old Jed came here a few days ago. He wanted to collect a few bits and pieces that he'd left behind. But he'd not be coming back, he said. Not without the lad. Terrible business that. I expect your mum and dad told you, didn't they?"

Davey Brown took me home in his car. I followed him into the kitchen, still dazed, trying to take in what he'd told me. Mum gave me a hot drink and I took it into the back room. I drew back the heavy curtains and looked out across the dark plain of the moors. Something outside was dripping, very slowly, very softly.

My mum came in and stood beside me. "Shall I tell you about Rab?"

Dread slowed the thumping of my blood. "Listen," I said. "It's thawing."

Mum touched my arm. "Dad and I didn't like to tell you. It was such a horrible thing. And anyway, you haven't seen him for months, have you?"

"Rab was my best friend," I said.

I didn't look at her while she was telling me. I didn't listen to her. I knew already what had happened to him. I listened instead to Rab and myself talking quietly together, sitting next to each other on The Edge before he showed me the frozen horse.

"*Everything's died.*"

"*It's the shortest day of the year. Everything's standing still. The sun, and the grass, and the streams, and the birds. Nothing's moving.*"

"*You'd think it was waiting for something.*"

"*There's nothing to wait for now. It's too late.*"

25

"Rab was killed a few weeks ago," my mum was
saying. "He stole a ride on somebody's horse, and it took
fright and threw him. He died on midwinter's day.
The longest night of the year."

The dripping from the roof had turned into a trickle.
I could see it coursing down the outside of the window;
ice running free again. Tomorrow the Downpour would
crack and burst and gush back to life.

But I'd never see Rab again. I thought of him, urging
the black horse on over the moors, riding free, laughing.
That's the way I want to remember him.

Ghost Galleon

1 The open sea

My home is on farmland, in the flat fens of East Anglia. They say that many years ago my fields were sea, and tides rose and fell over the fields that sway with wheat and in the groves that are now tight with trees.

I discovered this when I was 12 years old and staying on holiday in this very house that now belongs to me, but which used to belong to my grandfather. It was at that same time that I discovered that my name, Charles Oliver, is not English but Spanish: Carlos Olivarez. But the story of how I came to have this name, and how I learnt the truth of it, is almost beyond belief.

It happened soon after I came to the house. I'd asked my grandfather if the Oliver family had always lived in that part of the country. Grandad didn't answer me at first; he seemed to be weighing the question up. And then he said, "If you're asking that, then I think it's time I moved you up to the little bedroom at the front of the house. Just for a bit."

He had that way about him, that made him seem full of unfathomable secrets – people say I have that way with me, too. Anyway, I didn't ask him anything more, and he didn't tell me, but that night my sleeping things were moved right up to the top floor of the house into the little bedroom that Grandad said he'd slept in when he was a boy.

There was nothing special about this room. I didn't like it much. It smelt damp, and it was dark and dusty. I had the feeling that no one had slept in it for years – maybe not since Grandad was my age – 60 years back. The window looked out on to a grove of beech trees, and beyond that, miles and miles of fields, and the long, dark horizon of the east.

It was because it faced east that I woke up so early next morning, with the first streak of dawn pushing itself like needles into my eyes. It must have been about 4 o'clock. I couldn't get back to sleep again and I lay in bed looking at the way the strange light cast reflections like ripples on my wall. I could hear the wind sighing, and it was a comforting sort of sound to lie in bed and listen to, even at that unearthly hour. Regular, gentle, hushing, with a to and fro heave to it. A rhythm. A kind of breathing; like the sea.

It *was* the sea!

I ran across to the window and leant out. There was still hardly any light to see by, only that first pale streak, but the gleam of it stretched a sort of path over something that was dark and moving, rolling, slow and steady, with here and there ghostly flecks of white.

My sense told me that what I could hear was the wind moving across the field of wheat, but my heart thudded in my throat with excitement and fear and told me that it was the sea. Yet the trees were there, black, between me and the skyline. I could hear the waves through the creaking of their tall trunks.

Suddenly, I realised that one of the trunks – no, two, three – three of the trunks were moving. They came gliding behind the pattern of the trees, and my racing heart stood still. Clear as anything, I saw the masts and rigging of a sailing ship.

Even then I didn't realise how massive a ship it was till it came properly into view. I saw that it had many decks and towered out of the water like a huge floating castle.

It had three or four masts, each with its own cross-spars and sails. I saw it in silhouette, blacker than a shadow against the light, but so clear that all the tight ropes of its rigging traced a pattern like lace from spar to spar, like a cradle of fine web. And yet it was enormous. I'd seen pictures of ships like that. It was a ship of war of 500 years ago.

It was a galleon.

I raced down the stairs and out of the house, my pyjama jacket flapping open. My thudding steps sent rabbits scudding across the grass, white tails bobbing like flashes of light.

The sun was flooding up now, glaring out not across sea, but the fields I'd always known.

A harsh cry, like a sob, caught my attention, and I saw a great, grey-white bird lift its heavy wings and drift slowly across the line of the sun, and away out of sight.

"Heron!" I shouted after it in disappointment, and back came its sad cry.

2 The return of the heron

At breakfast I played safe.

"Grandad, I had a funny dream last night."

"Did you, Charlie? What was it about?"

"I dreamt that the fields behind the trees were the sea."

"Did you now?" said Grandad. "Well that wasn't such a funny dream. Hundreds of years ago most of this land *was* sea. All this farmland was reclaimed from the sea. If this house had been here then, the waves would have come crashing over the doorstep."

I buttered my toast carefully. *Had* I known that already? I was sure I hadn't. But had I dreamt it?

I decided to pretend I wasn't much interested in the answer to my next question.

"Would there have been galleons?" I asked carelessly.

"Oh, yes. It's said, Charlie, that this coast was the route of the Spanish Armada, in 1588. They came right up here and over the top of Scotland."

Long after Grandad left the table, I still sat there, smoothing and smoothing a skin of butter over my cold toast.

I kept my secret to myself. That night I couldn't wait to get back up to my bedroom. I pushed open the window and leant out, staring as the gloom gathered the sky into its darkness, till there was nothing more to see.

I didn't know I'd gone to sleep till I was pulled awake by a cry coming from outside. I caught the surge and sigh that I'd heard the night before. A gust of air brought in a cool dampness. There was a tang to it, sharp and unmistakeable, with salt on its breath. It was the smell the wind brought with it when the tide was coming in.

And then I heard the cry again.

Again I raced down the stairs. I thudded down the track to where I knew the trees would be. But light was beginning to come in, just a glow that was pale gold. I knew then with a rush of fear that there *were* no trees, and that the cold sting on my cheeks was the fling of spray. I turned to look back, and saw that the big old farmhouse was gone. In its place was a cottage or hut, no bigger than one of our barns. But there wasn't time to even think about that.

Water was lapping round my bare feet. I heard a massive creaking and the bark of voices. I could just make out an enormous bulk moving somewhere far out in front of me, with little lights swinging on it, and into the line of the day's first light came gliding, first the prow, then the hull, masts and all, and rigging and straining sails, of a galleon.

I saw the silk banners streaming scarlet and silver and gold, and the white sails arched like wings in flight, and the lettering picked out in gold: *La Garza*. It was Spanish. A cloud dulled the sunlight and all I could make out then were lanterns gleaming like animals' eyes, and the dark shape gliding quiet as death over the fields of my grandad's farm.

There was the cry again. This time I knew what it was. A child was in the water, and he was shouting for help.

I was a good swimmer, so my next action was completely instinctive. I never even stopped to think about the weirdness of the situation, but waded out into the sea of nearly 500 years ago, up to my knees, up to my thighs, and then plunged in.

"*Ay! Socorro!*" the voice cried.

I'd no idea then what the words meant, but they'll stay in my memory for the rest of my life. It's Spanish. Help, it means.

"*Socorro!*"

Gulls' cries drowned his voice. I kept losing sight of the bobbing head, and the sea wanted to drag me down. But at last I did reach him and he seemed to be half dead.

I managed to hold him up somehow with my arm hooked under his armpit while I struggled to pull off my pyjama top. I'd been told at school how to make a kind of balloon out of it, but I never thought the day would come when I'd have to, or be able to.

I kept going under with him, and the sea choked every breath I took, but with both my arms around the boy, I paddled for shore. I'd never swum so far before. I wanted to give up the battle and just leave go of him and let myself drift away into sleep.

My body touched land at last, but I wasn't yet out of the sea. We were shored on a sandbank a few yards from the beach. Waves kept pulling me back, and I hadn't the strength to heave us any further.

I wouldn't have made those last few metres if a woman hadn't come running out of the little thatched cottage. She waded into the sea with her long skirts billowing round her, and dragged us out of the water.

"Mercy on us, lad. What's this you've caught?" she said in the strange accent of long ago. She knelt by the boy, marvelling at his olive skin and his black hair and lashes, his strange clothes.

"He's Spanish," I panted, struggling to sit up. "Can you help him?"

"Help a Spaniard?" She spat into the sand. She cocked her head sideways as though she couldn't make me out. "That's asking me to help the enemy!"

I crawled over to the boy and lifted his head up.
He coughed, and water streamed from his mouth.

"What a poor wretch he is!" The woman wrapped her
shawl round his shivering body.

He opened his eyes. He looked terrified.

"You're all right," I said. "You'll be all right now."

"Leave him be!" the woman said. "He'll not understand thy talk."

His eyes flitted from me to the woman and back again. He shook his head.

"I'm Charlie," I said, pointing to myself, "Charles Oliver. You?" I pointed to him.

"*Yo Carlos Olivarez!*" the boy answered.

"It's the same name!" I said.

"*Lo mismo,*" agreed the boy, and we stared as if we had always known each other.

The woman had moved away from us and was standing with her hand shielding her eyes from the sun, looking out to sea. "Methinks the boy will not return to Spain," she said. "See how his ship flies home!"

Far away on the horizon now, right into the sunlight, the galleon scudded in full sail with all her banners streaming.

The boy Carlos pulled himself up with a terrible cry of grief. "*La Garza! La Garza!*"

I turned my eyes away at last from the retreating ship. The boy was gone, and the woman with him, and the little thatched cottage. I was standing on grass, in our field, with our farmhouse behind me. The field sloped down to the grove of beech trees and beyond that, field after field stretched out to the horizon. A great winged heron rose into the sunlight with its sad and solitary cry.

In a daze I went back into the house. This time I knew I must tell Grandad everything. I was scared to go back to bed in case I fell asleep and came to think of all these strange things as a dream. But my pyjamas were wet and my skin tasted of salt and I could still remember the weight of the drowning boy in my arms.

As soon as Grandad was awake I told him my story. He took it in his quiet way, not surprised.

"Well, you've answered your question, Charlie. You asked me if our family had always lived here, and the answer is – yes. Since the time of the Spanish Armada. The first member of our family to live here was a Spaniard."

"Carlos Olivarez."

Grandad nodded. "And now you know more than I ever knew. You know how he came here, and why he stayed."

"He was a ship's boy off a Spanish galleon, and he fell overboard, and was rescued by an English boy and a fisherwoman." I remembered the look on the woman's face when she decided to pity the enemy and take him into her house.

If she hadn't ... if Carlos hadn't been rescued from the sea ... he would have drowned. None of us would have been born. Not me, nor my dad, nor my grandad, nor any of the long line stretching back to the 16th century. The thought of it all made me dizzy.

"Grandad, did the same thing happen to you when you slept up in that room? Is that why you wanted me to sleep up there?"

He shook his head. "I thought I heard the sea when I slept up there. It puzzled me, but I never saw it. Your dad heard it too, and as a child it frightened him. My father told me he saw the sea, and heard the creakings of an enormous ship of some sort. And we've all heard the same cry out there at dawn. I don't think anyone ever saw the ghost galleon before you did, Charlie. And I don't suppose anyone will, now. It won't come back."

"Why not?" I asked. In spite of all the terrible happenings of the night before, I felt I wanted to see that beautiful ship again. I felt as if I belonged to it, and that the galleon belonged to me.

"Why should it?" said Grandad. "The ghost boy has been rescued. No need now for the ghost galleon to come in search of him."

I knew Grandad was right. "I think I'll go down tomorrow morning all the same," I said, "just in case it's there."

"You'll see something, but it won't be the galleon. I'll come with you, Charlie."

Well, I did go down with Grandad next morning, and what I saw filled me with a strange sadness, as if I was remembering it from long ago.

I saw the distant fields of wheat surging gold like the sea with sunlight on it. I heard the wind sighing in the branches of the trees, like the breathing of waves. And I heard that strange, sad, half-human cry. The heron lifted its great heavy wings and drifted out slowly towards the line of the sun, and what I saw then wasn't a bird any longer.

It was Carlos Olivarez' galleon. *La Garza. The Heron.* It was arching back its sails like huge white wings and it was flying home on the winds of time to Spain. Without him.

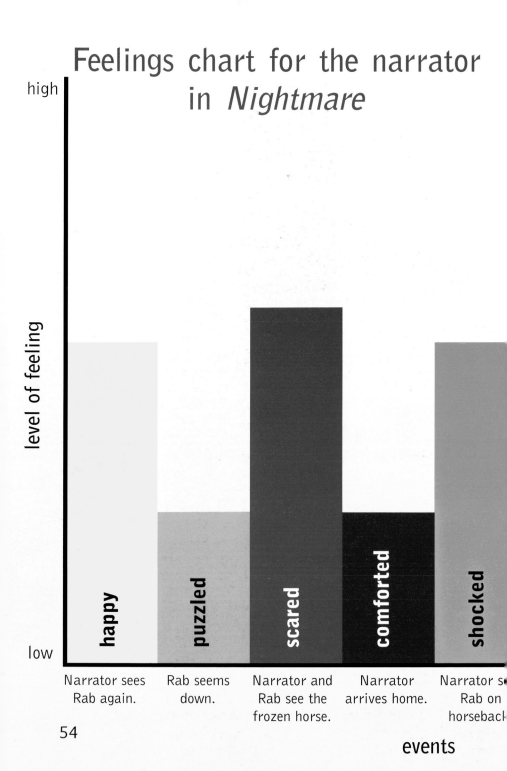

Feelings chart for the narrator in *Nightmare*

high

low

level of feeling

happy — Narrator sees Rab again.

puzzled — Rab seems down.

scared — Narrator and Rab see the frozen horse.

comforted — Narrator arrives home.

shocked — Narrator s... Rab on horseback...

events

54

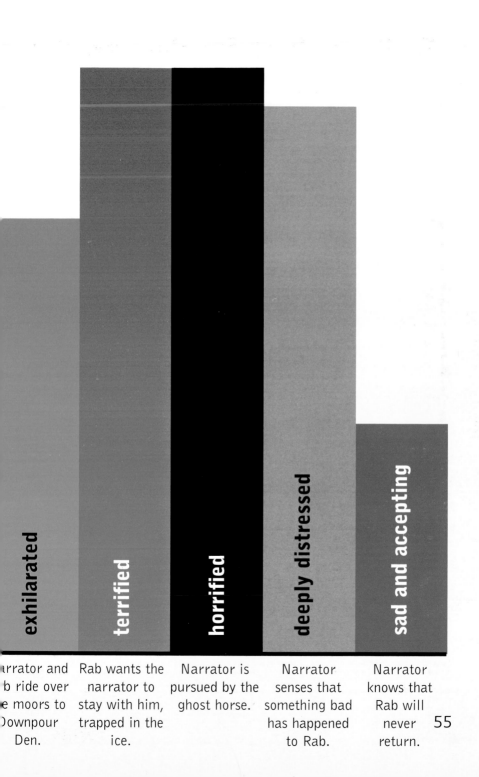

exhilarated	**terrified**	**horrified**	**deeply distressed**	**sad and accepting**
Narrator and Rab ride over the moors to Downpour Den.	Rab wants the narrator to stay with him, trapped in the ice.	Narrator is pursued by the ghost horse.	Narrator senses that something bad has happened to Rab.	Narrator knows that Rab will never return.

55

Ideas for guided reading

Learning objectives: understand underlying themes, causes and points of view; sustain engagement with longer texts using different techniques; use a range of oral techniques to present engaging narratives

Curriculum links: Citizenship: Living in a diverse world

Interest words: desolate, fossilised, clamour, shards, sinewy, languorous

Resources: ICT, musical instruments, digital voice recorder

Getting started

This book can be read over two or more guided reading sessions.

- Share an example of a nightmare with the children. Invite children to recount some examples of nightmares that they have had.

- Read the front and back covers together. Predict what may happen to the two friends in the first story. Discuss the themes that may be raised, e.g. *friendship, fear, loyalty*.

Reading and responding

- Focus on the first story. Read to p5 to the children. Ask them to listen with their eyes closed.

- Help children to respond to the story. Ask them to make notes about what they can see in their mind's eye when you are reading, to list any questions that they have about the characters/story, and to list any other stories, films or events that the story reminds them of.

- Make brief character sketches of Rab and the narrator based on what is told and what the reader can infer.

- Ask children to read independently to the end of the story, p26.